T0162668

Poems
from the Heart
Reflections of Love

C. D. Boyden

Order this book online at www.trafford.com
or email orders@trafford.com

Most Trafford titles are also available at major online book retailers.

Print information available on the last page.

ISBN: 978-1-4907-4816-0 (sc)
ISBN: 978-1-4907-4818-4 (hc)
ISBN: 978-1-4907-4817-7 (e)

Library of Congress Control Number: 2014917839

Trafford rev. 02/24/2015

 www.trafford.com

North America & international
toll-free: 1 888 232 4444 (USA & Canada)
fax: 812 355 4082

Contents

My Wish 1

Love is… 3

Someday 5

Not all Moms Are Like You 7

Once 9

The Key 10

One Last Time 12

The Road 14

If I Could Be Anything 16

The Sea 18

Love Will Always Be 21

Trail of Tears 24

Teacher Teacher 27

We Stood Together 29

Walk with Me 32

A Path for Two 37

US 39

For Just one Day 41

Remember Whens 44

No Matter What 46

My Heart Next to Yours 50

Mr. Tambourine Man 52

Memories 55

Let it Go! 59

The Simple Things...61

I Dream Your Name.. 63

One For Me... 66

Eclipse of the Moon 69

Don't Let Go..71

Cowboy 74

A Book of Love..76

Angels Walk Among Us................................. 82

Angel with No Name...................................... 85

Walk in the Sand...87

Tonight in Your Dreams 90

With You.. 93

When I Meet You...96

The Road Left Behind.................................... 98

The One for Me... 100

Sometimes..103

To Ride with You...105

Forever 110

A Rose for You!... 112

Chapter in Life.. 114

A Heart that Is True.......................................120

Adore..122

I Wish For You 125

Cold without You...127

Days..129

I Give to You 131

More 133

One Last Thought 135

My Purpose Is You 137

Towel Meant for Two 139

Wonder When 141

King and Queen 143

One... 145

Dad... 148

Days Gone By 151

You Were My Dream 154

A Day Alone 156

You Take Me There.. 158

You Didn't Have to Be 160

Found You 162

Her Man to Find 164

Your Love I Find... 166

Reasons Not to Run … 169

My Wish

If I had one thing in the world to keep with me, I'd choose to hold your hand through all eternity. The warmth within as I hold you close, holding hands, fingers folding over closed. The space between my fingers meant for yours. To feel my heart beat with yours. Love, every tear I've ever cried you've captured. Our fingers interlaced, you calm my racing heart when it beats out of time. The tenderness shared between us. To show you so, it's then I realize no harm would ever come as long as we hold hands forever. We walk hand in hand down life's winding road. For you to always feel all the love I have to give. To have you in my life completely, always and forever, would fulfill me!

Love is...

Love is
unconditional support for your partner always and forever.

Love is
to share all moments in life together.

Love is
to give to each other with out asking anything in return,
never to take without appreciation.

Love is
to give and receive, only to return it twofold so that you
build on the received, making your love and relationship
stronger every day.

Love is
respect for one another and adoration of the other partner, always building on the little things, making a partnership stronger for the big things.

Love is
sharing the good and the bad together, supporting each other no matter what.

Love is
she is always the only woman in the room!

Love is
to treat her as my equal, but special like no other; to always give her all my love unconditionally, forever and always; never allowing for doubt of how much I love her, letting her know how special she is to me each and every day and how loved she will always be.

Someday

I created Someday just for you.
It's not Sunday, it's not Monday.
You can't find it on the calendar:
It's not a day of the week.
It's not an hour or two.
It's the time I share with you.

For when I am with you every day is Someday,
The day I reserve for two.
There is never enough time to share with you,
So I created Someday just for you.

There are only 24 hours in a day,
7 days in a week,
365 days in a year.
There is never enough time to share with you,
So I created Someday just for you.

For time stands still when I am with you,
Someday is your day only for you:
No morning alarm,
No work,
Only play on Someday.

Someday is time spent together,
Time with no end,
No worries no problems,
Create memories for hours on end.
For time stands still
On Someday.

It's neither day or night,
No clock on the wall.
Someday is filled with smiles and laughter,
For Your day is Someday.

Someday is you in my heart,
Time with no end,
Together forever,
For Someday will come again.

Not all Moms Are Like You

Not all moms are like you.
I thought all moms were like you—
So not true.
It always nice to hear an *I love you.*

Not all moms are like you.
Some swear,
Some drink,
Some stay out too late.

Not all moms are like you.
Some forget a hug or maybe two;
Some forget to say I love you—
So not like you.

Not all moms are like you.
Some forget to cook a meal,
Or maybe two,
But no one cooks as good as you.

Not all moms are like you.
Some pack lunches,
Some forget to;
You always made enough for two.

Not all moms are like you.
You kept us warm, you kept us fed.
You kept a roof over our head.
You put us first, you never forgot to.

Not all moms are like you.
Always a hug,
Always a smile,
Always the one to share a little style.

Not all moms are like you.
You gave us strength,
You gave us courage.
You always gave us an *I love you.*

Not all moms are like you.
We do our best because of you:
Hope to make you proud,
Because we love you.

Once

Once you stole my heart.
Once was first;
Once is all I want;
Once is all I need.

Once I held your hand;
Once I kissed your lips;
Once I heard your voice;
Once I looked in your eyes.

Once was always;
Once is forever;
Once in my heart;
Once locked forever.

Once it starts,
Once never ends.
Once begins our hearts:
Once together, connected forever.

The Key

A love lost, a love found,
The love that is yours,
Lost in yourself.
When you look,
You never find.

When lost in yourself,
The one you love,
The one love will always be
No such thing as can't be.

Eyes are not the key—
Trust in faith,
See with your heart,
For in your heart is the key.

In the dark you follow the path,
The path you can't see,
Follow your heart,
Never to stray.

To love the one you love—
For love finds you.
Only love can make it true.
For the love is within you.

Once was lost,
But never gone.
Locked away,
To find the key.

Who is the one who holds the key?
Look in side
For you will find
The one and only key.

The love that was never gone,
Here it sits,
Now it is found,
The lock for the key.

Now it comes to be,
The lock is found.
Try the key,
Open the heart love comes to be.

One Last Time

A full moon shines,
A star in the sky!
A kiss in the night,
A sparkle in your eye!

We live our love
Day to day,
Dawn to dusk,
Dark in the night.

Never alone,
You for me,
The one,
The one meant for me.

Keep you steady,
Hold your hand,
Pick you up,
When you are down.

Never far,
Always near,
Never to fear,
To hold you dear.

Never to leave,
For it was true,
True to you,
Meant for you, meant for me.

Don't let go,
Hold me close,
For I will shine,
One last time.

The Road

Wishing on stars,
Roads less traveled with no end,
On the horizon yet again,
Tomorrow may never end.

Travel the road,
Wondering what tomorrow will bring,
Looking for answers,
As there is none so it seems.

The road rolls on—
An empty tank,
Never to be full,
A heavy load to leave behind.

A winding road yet ahead,
Another turn,
One more hill yet to crest,
Yet to stop.

The roads grow long
With no end.
My eyes grow tired,
Yet to see.

Where is the fire
Yet to be.
Many miles left behind,
Many more lay ahead.

A destination yet to find:
No map for you,
No wrong turns,
One road yet to lead me to you.

One day maybe to be,
Hand in hand, We will see.
Roads less traveled together
You and me!

C. D. Boyden

If I Could Be Anything

If I could be anything,
I would be your tear:
To be born in your eyes,
Live down your cheek,
Die on your lips.

If I could be anything,
I would be your air:
To kiss your lips,
With each breath,
A tender touch never to forget.

If I could be anything,
I would be the sunlight
That shines on your face:
To feel the warmth of your skin,
Never to forget the beauty within.

If I could be anything,
I would be your sustenance:
To nourish your love,
Make you strong,
Give you life.

If I could be anything,
I would be your night:
To give you rest,
To share your dreams,
Give you hope.

If I could be anything,
I would be your tomorrow:
To dream of dreams,
To share today,
To remember when.

If I could be anything,
I would be your everything:
Your heart, your soul,
Your one, your only,
Your best friend.

If I could be anything,
I would be the heart to your soul:
For you are my everything,
My wish, my dream.

The Sea

A Goddess you will be to me:
To hold you dear to me;
My Girl you will be.
On our way to the sea

Your heart to belong to me:
Let me hold your hand
As I lead you to the sand.
On our way to the sea.

My love, my life:
To belong to you.
My one, my only.
On our way to the sea.

Sunsets to see:
Not just a dream,
Forever to be you and me.
On our way to the sea.

No dream too big:
For you and me,
A team to be.
On our way to the sea.

A dream come true, just to find you:
Part of me has always been part of you;
Now to find me within you.
On our way to the sea.

A love to share:
Together we will see
The best is yet to be
On our way to the sea.

A day with you, or an hour or two:
It's never enough to share with you;
Forever will have to do
On our way to the sea.

My heart to give:
A life of love
Together we live
On our way to the sea.

C. D. Boyden

To love you tomorrow:
Just like today,
To wake beside you
On our way to the sea

Together we have forever:
Every day gets better;
To love you forever
On our way to the sea!

Love Will Always Be

You can't go back,
You can't change the past,
Past but a memory,
Good or bad.

Move forward,
Don't look back,
Memories already made,
They made you.

Don't forget *remember when's*.
Dream big,
Love bigger,
Dance in the rain.

Take a ride,
Once in a while.
Breath deep,
Worry less.

Hold hands,
Give your heart when you can.
Take long walks,
Stand in the rain.

Risk is reward,
Be true to you.
As she is to you,
Nothing ventured nothing gained.

Wake up happy
next to you.
Make your choices.
Then I choose you.

Remember: say *I love you*.
I hope I always do.
Hold on to all that is dear.
And I love you just for you.

When you find love,
Hold it near.
Breathe your love.
For Love is free.

Love will never leave
The one for thee.
Love will always set you free.
Together you and me ... love will always be!

Trail of Tears

I look at you,
What do I see?
I wonder… what it is you see?
A trail of tears for you to find.

It's not because of you,
It's not because of me.
From time gone by,
Trail of tears left behind.

Once a heart full of love
For someone like thee.
I shed a tear or two … or maybe three.
Trail of tears for you to find.

A heart with soul,
A lost love to find,
A hurt or two left behind.
Trail of tears for you to find.

To love the one,
No hurt or pain,
Once again left behind.
Trail of tears for you to find.

My love to give,
No one to receive.
Hopes of you a gift to give,
Trail of tears for you to find.

An empty heart yet to fill,
The days pass by.
I close my eyes.
Trail of tears for you to find.

To dream of you,
To hold your hand,
With hopes of you.
Trail of tears for you to find.

To start my day,
Share a kiss just for you,
To share a smile when I think of you.
Trail of tears left just for you.

I start each day
With hopes of you,
To share me with you.
Trail of tears for you to find.

Not only in my dreams
To see your face,
To hold you close.
Trail of tears for you to find.

The trail of tears I have left behind
Just for you, some day soon—
For you will find,
My gift to give;
In our hearts we will live!

Teacher Teacher

Teacher Teacher,
We see you each morning.
You give us smiles,
You give us joy.
We gain your knowledge
To be good girls and boys.

Teacher Teacher,
You task the plan,
You grade the papers,
You take us by the hand.

Teacher Teacher,
You make the rules,
You teach us great lessons.
We take your tests,
We move on to the next.

Teacher Teacher,
This is all new.
The words in books, you help us understand
So we pass your next test.

Teacher Teacher,
We will do our best,
For you taught us well
Now to move to a higher test.

We enter the world.
We look back
With fond memories.
Teacher Teacher,
We don't forget.

We Stood Together

It seemed like yesterday we stood together.
We stood together for the first time.
We stood in fields,
Looked at the stars,
Shared our dreams.

After all these years,
My dreams stood with you.
I never dreamt it would be.
Who would have known it would end this way?

The stars brought me to you,
The woman in my life.
I was the man in your dreams.
I tried to be the husband you wanted me to be.

The love we shared,
You leave me now.
But it will always be
You and me.

I never said goodbye,
But that's ok.
You know now it was you and me.
For that… it will always be.

I take you now
Under my arm.
In my heart
You will always be.

The love we shared,
You in my heart.
That's the way it will always be.
Don't forget me—
I won't forget you!

The tears we shared,
The smiles, the laughter,
The small things should have never been
That kept us apart, never again.
We shared a life the best it could have been.

Remember when we stood together.
We stood together for the first time
Out in field hand in hand.
A kiss goodnight,
A memory shared that will never end.

Walk with Me

Beauty like yours
Comes from within.
A sister to me you will always be,
So come walk with me.

A picture not yet taken,
A picture of you to always hold.
In my heart you will always be,
So come walk with me.

A memory of you,
Memory from within.
No camera, no lens,
To walk with you for hours on end.

When I come to see you,
I bring a special hug, maybe two,
Hopes to see you smile,
So I may walk with you.

Day or night, by your side,
To hold your hand
For a moment or two,
So I may walk with you.

Big smile from me to you,
To sit by your side,
A kiss on the cheek,
As I walk with you.

We fight together,
Never to lose,
Only to win.
We walk together for hours on end.

Memories we made,
Memories we shared,
In good times and in bad,
We walk together, we always have.

The picture of you
Will never fade.
Time stands still
When I walk with you.

I hold you dear,
A spot in my heart,
As special as you,
So I may walk with you.

I hold you dear,
From me to you,
A special hug holds us together,
As I walk with you.

A picture I made
Special for you,
As sisters always do,
So I may walk with you.

Tell me a story or maybe two.
Who is the boy
That will always love you?
As we walk, I will tell you.

A heart so pure,
A soul so true,
A sister to love,
When I walk with you.

I touch your hand,
I hear your voice,
I hold you dear,
When I walk with you.

I picked you up
When you were down,
As I love my sister
Like no one else can.

A bowl of soup,
Made just for two,
Made with love,
So I may walk with you.

I tucked you in,
With my two hands,
As sisters do,
As I walk with you.

A kiss goodnight,
I hold your hand,
Forever you will be ...
My sister, to walk with me.

A Path for Two

A path for two,
A winding road,
I wonder when,
I wonder who.

For those who search,
One will find,
To find the one,
The one we seek!

A path to cross,
For who's to know,
When it will be,
For you to find.

A day to wake,
A day to live,
The day for us
For tomorrow exists.

For you to find,
That day will be
Hearts together,
For us to live.

The one to seek
To fill my heart,
With love for you,
Let it be.

The path for you,
The path for me,
The path we seek,
The path will be you for me.

US

Us, you and me,
One day I hope to see
One you just for me,
A wonder yet to be.

Us just two,
Where are you, come to me,
One me, one you,
Both to be.

One us from you and me,
To meet by chance,
A smile, a glance,
A fleeting chance.

A note from you to me,
My reply just for you.
Never new, how it would be;
How wonderful you are, already to me.

Feelings never felt,
Two hearts to open,
Not to let go,
As we trust in us forever more.

Forever would be
The moment we kiss.
Holding hands,
A ring to represent, us to be.

The sound of surf,
The sun sinks low.
Your hands in mine,
A question for you and one for me.

Two *I do's*,
The moment brings you to me,
The perfect you for the perfect me,
The perfect us we will always be.

For Just one Day

To love you for just one day,
I would give up power and fame;
To hold you near, to love you dear,
For just one day.

To love you for just one day,
No one to judge,
No one but us,
You and me we would be.

To love for just one day,
To know all of you for just one day,
Your open heart next to mine,
You for me, me for you,
For just one day.

To love with no fear,
To trust and not hear,
To share all of you with all of me,
For just one day.

To shed your fears,
To save your tears,
To hold you near,
Love for you is always dear.

Give all of me to all of you,
Give you my heart
With all my love,
In just one day.

A day turns to two,
Time starts a life with you,
A lifetime of love shared with you,
A lifetime of memories shared for two.

When you're near for just one day,
A lifetime happens in just one day.
To love you once,
To love you for just one day.

You by my side for just one day.
One day with you starts love for two.
One day starts forever, forever never ends.
I will love you forever, in just one day!

Remember Whens

My first remember when:
A moment or two
Made for you,
The day I met you.

To grow together,
To love together,
Share together,
Remember when.

The days turn to nights,
Nights to day.
Today turns to tomorrow.
Remember when.

Soon yesterday remains,
The weeks to months,
Months of season, now years—
To always remember when.

Turn to you my dear,
Beauty so rare,
For you, my dear,
Will be my remember when.

Tomorrow is memories to make.
Today is memories to share.
Yesterday is memories made.
You will always be the one to remember our when's.

No Matter What

The who's, the where's, the when's,
Near or far,
No matter what,
As your friend.

All the unknowns
In life's winding road,
No matter what,
You're my friend.

Pick you up when you fall down,
Dust you off,
Maybe hold your hand.
No matter what you're my friend.

An introduction to good friends,
Share a glass of wine,
A bottle or two … probably more!
No matter what, I've made good friends.

You take a walk in hopes to see.
You stop to pray to the trees.
You find your path in hopes to see.
No matter what, a friend you will be.

Now I lay you down to sleep.
A kiss on the lips,
Or maybe three.
I hold you close,
Sweet dreams for you and for me.

The one and only
You are to me.
Sparkling eyes
Each time I see.
I smile inside for only you to see.

A rainy day
Made for two.
An adventure we will share.
Just Me with you.

We share stories of you and me
Happy and sad
Good friends we will be.
No matter what till the end.

A visit with family,
A new meeting for me.
What a great place to be,
A great friend next to me.

To dream of you each day through
In hopes of seeing you.
Make you smile, make you laugh,
No matter what, a friend to me.

Life's every twist and turn,
Life's ups and downs,
No matter what,
I hope to be there with my friend.

To see you happy,
When no one else can.
A heart so pure,
A smile so true,
To burn our light all the night.

Give you comfort
In my sight.
Kiss your lips now no one else can.
A special place next to me.

Beauty so rare
Inside of you,
Amazing and wonderful,
It is all just you!

All the hugs, all the kisses,
All yours.
No matter what … you will be…
A special friend always to me!

C. D. Boyden

My Heart Next to Yours

I wish my heart were next to yours,
My hand in yours,
When I kiss you goodnight,
To lay my heart next to yours.

With hopes of together
We start each day,
A smile, a kiss, a smack on the lips,
My heart next to yours.

The smile on your face,
The smell of your hair,
The touch of your hand,
My heart next to yours.

We start our day,
We are on our way,
We both go our separate ways,
But my heart is always yours.

Every breath I take,
The ups and downs,
The highs and lows,
I feel my heart next to yours.

A thought, a wish,
A daydream of you,
All day I think of you,
My heart is always next to you.

As the day comes to a close,
I lock the doors,
My hand in yours,
My heart now next to yours.

Mr. Tambourine Man

Mr. Tambourine man,
You're a man with a heart,
You're a man with soul,
You're a man with music,
You want others to know.

You have words to speak,
You have ears to hear,
A smile within,
And inner glow,
Mr. Tambourine man.

You have peace in mind,
You play from your heart,
You play with your soul,
Mr. Tambourine man.

You don't speak words,
Your music is the key,
The words spill out,
But never a sound,
Only the music from
Mr. Tambourine man.

You dance with the ladies,
You make them smile,
The music is still the key,
To Mr. Tambourine man.

You want the world,
To see the music to your soul.
Your kind words not easily spoken,
Heard through the silence
With a magic glow,
Mr. Tambourine man.

You share your thoughts,
Your music overflows,
The kindness in your heart,
The sheerness of your soul,
Mr. Tambourine man.

Your magic touch,
Not everybody knows,
Your God's grace,
Your God's splendor,
Mr. Tambourine man, Mr. Tambourine man,
You are Mr. Tambourine man wherever you go!

Memories

Pictures upon pictures,
Snapshots in our minds of moments passing by,
Moments shared with friends,
Memories forever kept.

Deep in our hearts,
In the back of our minds all held dear,
Family friends sharing special moments,
Fond memories forever kept.

Love and laughter shared,
A kind word, warm smile,
Good food, fine wine, family time,
Fond memories forever kept

A chocolate kiss,
A bottle of Friken
Made in Germany ... nonetheless!
Fond memories shared.

Across the miles
We gather here to share this time
With special friends near and dear.
We learn new languages.
Once again a memory kept.

You open your hearts,
You open your home,
You have given more than you could know,
Love and laughter once again.
Memories held dear forever kept.

Thank you is not enough.
With friendship and love,
Kindness you show.
Fond memories I will always know.

A walk on the beach,
Surf and sand at our feet,
Gentle breeze and birds I see,
More fond memories for all of us to see.

We ride the bikes,
We share good cheer,
Laughter is dear,
Good memories again … held dear.

A Miller Lite, a Jell-O shot or two;
If that's not enough,
A shot of Friken will do!
Hopes to remember it all too!

A Moi-Cheri,
A Duplo or two,
Crème Nugget AuxChocolate,
Yummy memories of all of you!

A gift from you to me,
As friendship should be,
Friends like you,
Create grand memories of all of you.

Little girl hugs,
And pony rides,
The cowgirl princess,
Fond memories of you.

We stand at the door,
Big hugs to share,
A sad good bye.
Mountains of fond memories made because of all of you!

Let it Go!

All are angels,
Some are demons.
Open your heart.
Let it go.

Try to hang on—
Hold on now,
Not too tight.
Let it go.

Time has come,
Never alone,
To find our way.
Let it go.

The road to be travelled,
For I am with you,
The time will come.
Let it go.

A ride alone,
A shot of Jack,
Never look back.
Let it go.

Pray to God,
Angels with you,
Demons behind.
Let it go.

To ride the wind,
Music to my soul,
My spirit will be.
Let it go.

Time will tell,
A future before,
A heart with love.
Hard to let go.

The Simple Things

Life, it's the simple things;
To hold your hand,
To kiss your lips,
To say "I love you."

Begin my day…
Whisper your name in your ear,
This means I love you.
It's the simple things.

To hold your hand,
Touch your arm,
See you smile,
Simple thought of you.

A look at you from across the room,
To know your there,
To now you care.
It's the simple things.

To hold the door,
My hand on yours,
Fill your glass-
It's the simple things.

The things that bring me to you
A morning smile,
A wink, a nudge,
It's the simple things.

Good night kiss,
Lay you next to me,
The way it should be.
It's the simple things.

It's just me,
Just for you,
It's the simple things,
To say *I love you!*

When I say "I love you,"
It means I am grateful for you,
To never be without you.
You are my everything:
So it is, *I love you!*

I Dream Your Name

A thought, a wish,
A passing dream,
A happy thought of you,
When I dream your name.

I hear your words,
Dream of your smile,
The look in your eyes,
When I dream your name.

An angel in my heart
With no name,
Part of a dream,
I dream your name.

Many thoughts of you-
I always miss you.
I hear your voice
When I dream your name.

To whisper your name,
I dream to touch you,
I dream to hold you,
I dream your name.

Far from you,
Two hearts alone,
For us we will find,
I dream your name.

I make a wish,
To hold you close,
You next to me,
I dream your name.

Precious words shared,
Shared between two,
A heart meant for you,
I dream your name.

A heart like yours,
So dear and true,
My time now just for you,
I dream your name.

You give me hope,
Never to be alone,
Always together,
I dream your name.

With a heart like yours,
The time will come.
Our love to share;
I dream your name

Two hearts with love,
Filled as one,
For you will be next to me,
When I dream your name.

C. D. Boyden

One For Me

You are the one for me …
Your eyes will shine for the very first time,
Two hearts full of love,
For you and me.

Some day soon I bring a hug for you, maybe two.
To only know you for me,
I hope to find my one true love,
Maybe find you across the sea.

A journey planned I hope to find
The one for me,
A lifetime of dreams,
I will share with you.

See you smile,
To walk hand in hand,
Hold you close,
A dream come true,
Me for you.

One day I may find you,
The day to be,
Hopes of many for you and me,
Smiles and laughter for us to share.

May days never end,
The nights to share,
With you and me,
It will be.

Our eyes will meet,
A feeling so deep,
A first kiss,
In hopes we meet.

Two hearts, two souls,
Love to share,
A life to live,
May never let go.

C. D. Boyden

You may be
The one the one for me.
Tell me where you will be.
I will come for thee.

The day will come,
For you and me,
How happy we may be,
Love will find you and me.

To love, to share,
You to me,
Two to be,
You and me.

Love to be,
Forever together,
Maybe you will be the one for me,
Someday we shall see.

Eclipse of the Moon

A picture of you,
In my heart will shine,
My future yet to find,
Beneath the eclipse of the moon.

My heart races with thoughts of you,
A life with you, but a memory,
My future I see,
As I wish upon the stars.

The day fades to night,
Blue and silver shines bright,
My wish remains into the night,
Under the light of the moon.

The moon goes out,
All is dark,
A smile so bright, all to remain
I dream beneath the eclipse of the moon.

A destination unknown,
To see you there in my dreams,
I pray, I will find
With one wish,
To make the list.

The dreams carry on,
A life for two,
You, me … maybe three,
Under the light of the moon.

God looks down and holds my hand,
Leads me to you, in love we find,
You're my heart, you're my soul,
You're my dream under the eclipse of the moon.

Don't Let Go

Hold me tight, don't let go
As we travel down life's winding road.
Life's twists and turns brought me to you.
Don't let go.

Tonight will be me with you.
Meet me at the door,
Kiss hello.
Don't let go.

Thoughts of you and me,
You cast a spell.
My heart now yours.
Don't let go.

To hold you close,
To hear your voice,
To hear you say,
Don't let go.

A minute with you,
To steal your heart,
To have and to hold,
Don't ever let go.

Touch of your hand,
The smile on your face,
To melt my heart,
Don't let go.

Love at first sight,
My heart is yours,
It's not mine anymore,
Don't let go.

Only me with you,
The girl with my heart,
A dream come true,
Don't let go.

Now happy with you,
A memory made,
A love to share,
Don't let go.

Lost when apart,
I found you,
Even for a moment,
Don't let go.

A day, a week, a year,
All my time now for you,
A minute without you… is forever to me.
Don't let go.

Cowboy

The man beneath the hat they call Cowboy.
From his boots, to his buckle, to his hat,
He is heart, he is soul, he is determination.
We call him Cowboy.

The man with God in his heart,
A woman by his side,
Family on his mind.
He is Cowboy through and through.

His words ring commitment,
Honest to a fault.
His heart is gold.
He holds true to God.
He is Cowboy.

His true love he holds dear,
In his heart
She is diamonds,
She is gold
To the man they call Cowboy.

Or house is not a home without my Cowboy.
Home is my heart next to yours,
Next to her one true love,
Next to Cowboy.

The days are long, the nights are cold.
Lay me down,
Hold me close,
Cowboy come home, tuck me in.

Cowboy, all I need is you.
Be by my side.
She admires him, as she only knows
The man…
They call Cowboy!

C. D. Boyden

A Book of Love

Empty pages yet to fill
A book in my heart,
A story to tell,
A book of love.

You and me,
Someday to be,
My love to share,
With my love to be.

Beauty and Grace,
A life to build,
My love to give,
With my love I will live.

Dreams of you,
Yet to live.
I will find you,
Me to give.

Many prayers said,
If only God will give
Me to you,
A life to live,

With hopes of you,
A dream to live,
A smile from you,
With a wish to give.

Close your eyes,
Dream your dream,
Walk the isle,
Hand in hand.

Kiss for you,
Special from me, me to you,
Now we seal our deal,
Forever yet to live.

C. D. Boyden

As I look in your eyes,
Your soul I see,
Lips of red,
Soft as sand.

Long blond hair
To touch with my hand,
Heart of gold,
Precious as land.

Your love to give,
Mine to receive,
Ours to share,
Forever your man.

Days of laughter yet to come,
To rise and shine,
You will always find,
A love like mine is one of a kind.

By your side,
To sleep at night,
I dream of you,
Your husband I am.

My angel from heaven,
My saving grace,
You healed my heart,
Healed the pain,
That had always been.

You had the key,
You open the door,
Because of you,
My heart now yours.

Your love so true,
A love so pure,
With hopes,
To give it all back to you.

No price too high,
No gold to give,
My heart is yours,
As long as I live.

My life is not enough,
For I only have one to give,
Our lives to share,
Forever together.

This is our start,
Till the end,
No race to win,
A life to live.

A journey to begin,
Never too far,
I will always take you
To the stars.

You turn the key
To open my heart.
You're here to be, only with me.
Our love will always be.

Never to walk alone,
The space between your fingers,
Mine in yours,
Hand in hand.

You are the key
In my heart.
It's you for me.
Forever it will always be.

Angels Walk Among Us

Angels walk among us,
Step by step.
They are the ones
That we all know.

Angels walk among us.
They have heart,
They have soul,
They are inspiration.

Angels walk among us.
They keep us safe.
They keep our hearts warm.
They are dedication.

Angels walk among us.
They are our friends.
They answer our prayers.
They show us the way.

Angels walk among us,
A stranger with a smile,
An outreached hand,
A pick you up when you are down.

Angels walk among us.
God sends them down.
God keeps us safe
When angels come down.

Angels walk among us.
They keep a steady hand.
They keep the wheels turning.
They don't let us down.

Angels walk among us.
As we grow weary,
They keep our eyes open.
They help us see clearly.

Angels walk among us.
How do I know?
There is beauty,
Then there is you.

Angels are the ones
With a gentle hand
That never let us down,
A friend to the end.

To love and to laugh,
To smile, to frown,
To live and to die,
Never alone....
Angels walk among us.

Angel with No Name

A cowboy with no claim to fame,
Only hope,
An unsuspecting place,
He hopes to find his place.

An angel she appears,
She comes from above,
Lord brought her here,
Now in the cowboy's heart.

The angel holds the key,
The key to her heart.
He can't resist
Now to find the key.

An angel of beauty,
Lost for now,
Hope to be found,
It's left to fate.

C. D. Boyden

Once now found,
The cowboy prays.
Time ticks by.
Fate plays its hand.

She comes from behind,
Spreads her wings,
Dreams to find
A ride ahead.

To ride together,
A kiss to share
With the sound of a bell
To keep them safe.

The ride begins
With parts to play.
He plays his part.
He hopes to win her heart.

The cowboy prays
One day, with no good-byes,
Never to leave,
His angel always to be…

Walk in the Sand

As we walk in the sand,
We walk hand in hand.
Together our toes touch the sand,
Together prints left in the sand.

No fear, no hurt, no pain,
We have everything to gain.
Our life to live, our life to share,
We walk in the sand.

No tide too strong to wash them away,
My friend, my today, my tomorrow,
Our hands hold tight.
We walk in the sand.

You are my amazing grace.
When I see your smile light up your face,
You give me hope when you are near.
We walk in the sand.

C. D. Boyden

Holding each other's hand,
The sand shifts, tides change,
A pair of foot prints left behind.
We walk in the sand.

Never to let go of each other's hand,
We walk in the sand.
Where no others can,
We walk in the sand.

Inside our dreams,
Time now saved,
Sand in a bottle,
As we walk in the sand.

Time meant for you and me,
For forever we will be together.
We hold our hearts in each other's hands,
As we walk in the sand.

This life before us yet to be,
The sand between us still to see.
Answers now in the sand,
Not yet seen for you and me.

Footprints in the sand not yet seen,
A child's heart maybe will be.
They leave more footprints in the sand
Now because there are three.

A dream in the sand,
Still to hold hands.
My love for you will always be
Forever and ever we walk in the sand.

Tonight in Your Dreams

The day fades, now a memory.
Our future to find,
Our life to live,
Tonight in your dreams.

The night now starts
As you close your eyes
To dream of me
Tonight in your dreams.

I am there,
The one for you.
You dream of me
Tonight in your dreams.

I will be there to touch and to hold,
To keep you safe,
So I am told, now hold you tight,
Tonight in your dreams!

I am the one
You wish to see
I will meet you there
Tonight in your dreams.

The one for you always near,
But never far,
Close your eyes, see me there.
Tonight in your dreams.

With a kiss good night,
Your breath on my neck,
Your hand on my chest,
Tonight in your dreams.

Yet to find a heart so true,
Deep in your chest,
A heart filled with love just for you,
Tonight in your dreams!

To hold you close,
With a hug and a kiss,
A soft gentle touch,
Tonight in your dreams.

A picture of me,
Never to fade,
Never to hurt, feel no pain,
Tonight in your dreams.

Good night my love,
For I will find you
Where I last left you,
Tonight in your dreams!

With You

I want to be with you,
Only you to be with me,
Wake up next to you.
Every day to start with you.

Feel your touch,
The smile on your face,
Tomorrow is the day.
Every day is with you.

An ocean apart,
For I will come,
To be your world.
Every day is with you.

Under the moon
In front of the fire,
A bottle of wine we can share.
Every day is with you.

Every day is good enough,
Just to be with you,
Touch your soul.
Every day is with you.

The one in my heart,
The one in my soul,
Give me to you.
Every day is with you.

A loving place,
A place for two,
Every day to remember.
Every day is with you.

Just to hear you say,
"I love you,"
See your face.
Every day is with you.

My dream to dream
Every memory of you,
A time, a place.
Every day is with you.

To close my eyes,
To dream of you,
A dream to be, to be with you.
As every day now ends with you.

When I Meet You

How do you know?
Is this where it begins?
Just to share a laugh or two
When I meet you.

What will we do?
Maybe share a beer or two.
Here's a smile from me to you
When I meet you.

Just to hold your hand,
Hope to make you laugh,
Hope to never let you go
When I meet you.

What will you do?
What will you think?
Will I be everything for you
When I meet you.

Take a dare. Take a chance.
Will you set me free?
Maybe hang on to me
When I meet you.

When I see you,
Your smile, your face.
Beauty with no trace
When I meet you

In hopes to see,
Just to meet me,
Come ride with me,
When I meet you.

Now I am here,
Where are you,
As I dream of you,
When I meet you.

Still no you as the old year ends.
A New Year now to begin.
No New Year kiss.
Still I dream, I dream of you, for I will … I will find you!

C. D. Boyden

The Road Left Behind

Yet to find the road left behind,
A dream or two,
No worries for you,
The road left behind.

A ride with no end,
With thoughts and prayers,
Hopes and dreams,
The road left behind.

With my shield,
With my pride,
I push on to ride
The road left behind.

Tires touch the road,
Wind in my hair,
Calm soft breeze,
The road left behind.

The dotted line clear before,
In my mirror I leave behind
Many memories left unshared,
The road left behind.

In my mirror the sunsets behind,
Headlights point clear ahead,
Round each corner,
The road left behind.

Another adventure yet ahead,
Now for me as well as you,
Just to share a laugh with you,
The road left behind.

One day to share with you,
The roar of bikes,
The sound of pipes,
The road left behind.

Hopes and fears yet to appear,
A friend that is dear,
One day soon yet to appear,
I hope to ride, the road left behind.

C. D. Boyden

The One for Me

You're the one for me.
When I found you,
An adventure for two,
In God's good hands.

The girl I never new
Now is really true.
In hopes I would find you,
You're the one for me.

A heart not touched,
It comes from within,
My love to give.
You're the one for me.

The one I love,
The one I miss,
The one God made just for me.
You're the one for me.

You stole my heart;
It belongs to you,
Not just me.
You're the one for me.

I knew from the start,
A first hug,
Now not alone.
You're the one for me.

To walk hand in hand,
I see your soul,
My best friend.
You're the one for me.

The kiss of your lips,
Makes time stand still,
Day or night.
You're the one for me.

It's the things you do,
The look in your eye,
The touch of your hand.
You're the one for me.

The beauty within,
A heart to heal,
The patience of one man,
You're the one for me.

Magical bliss,
From our first kiss,
Joined at the lips,
You're the one for me.

One of a kind,
A gentle smile, a strong hand,
You hope to find a good man,
I am the one, just for you!
You're the one, just for me!

Sometimes

Sometimes it starts where it ends,
No beginning no end,
Just time in between.
Time is but a gift,
No finish no end.

A dollar to earn,
To buy a smile, a hug, and an *I love you*.
Time to spend
Would be payment enough.

Friends forever,
Family starts with us together,
Me and you,
For now just two.

Hopes to share
Every day and every night,
To share a sunrise,
Share a sunset.

We live each day,
We seize each moment,
Build memories,
Together shared

Time stand still when I hug you,
A hundred hugs to give just to you,
A thousand smiles from me to you,
Don't forget an *I love you* once in a while.

Hearts stand still
For those you love.
For with you always is forever.
Forever starts and never ends!

To Ride with You

A passing glance,
You caught my eye,
Not on the ride just by chance,
Just to ride with you.

A star so bright,
Yet you shine,
Your name unknown,
Just to ride with you.

A heart stands still,
To touch your hand,
To hear your name,
Just to ride with you.

A smile so true,
Eyes so bright,
A piece of my heart just for you,
Just to ride with you!

C. D. Boyden

Days go by,
To dream of you,
May I find you,
Just to ride with you.

I see your smile,
So vivid and true,
My heart holds on to hopes of you,
Just to ride with you.

To know you're near,
I count the days,
From day to day,
Just to ride with you.

No matter where,
No matter when,
Hope to find my best friend,
Just to ride with you.

The clock on the wall,
Time in my heart,
All stands still,
Just to ride with you.

Side by side,
On the back,
To know you're close,
Just to ride with you.

A heart next to mine,
To kiss your lips,
To hold you close,
Just to ride with you.

To see you clear,
The view so bright,
A memory to make,
Just to ride with you.

The one I thought never found,
To hold your hand,
Here by my side,
Just to ride with you.

In the sky,
Under the moon,
To see the stars as two best friends,
Just to ride with you.

I ride alone.
No hill too steep, yet I climb,
A winding road lay behind;
Just to ride with you.

Always close,
When I stop,
To see you smile,
Just to ride with you.

You to be first, never last,
A heart with soul,
Full of life, share the ride,
Just to ride with you,

A feeling deep as one never knows,
Yet to define the great unknown,
A path to unfold, yet to explore,
Just to ride with you.

A bump in the road,
My angel is yours,
To keep you safe,
Just to ride with you.

To ride again in my heart,
Love to give, yours to receive,
I ride alone.
I hope you will be "the one" to ride with me!

Forever

Forever with you,
Forever is made for two,
You and me together.
Forever is forever.

How long is forever?
Forever is not enough
For time spent with you.
I can't imagine forever without you.

Forever is the smile on your face,
You in my arms,
A kiss or two.
Forever doesn't exist without you.

Forever is not a place you can go;
It's a place in time,
A place in my heart.
Forever is reserved just for you.

Forever is you in my heart,
You on my mind.
Forever is… I miss you.
Forever doesn't exist without you.

Forever is time standing still.
For when I am with you,
Forever is not a day or an hour.
Forever is our time together.

Forever keeps us together.
Forever begins and never ends.
Love starts the beginning of forever.
My love for you will never end, always forever.

When you laugh, when you cry,
My love for you will always be.
Forever we will be together… always is forever.
I will love you … forever and ever!

A Rose for You!

Pink or blue,
Just for you,
Indeed it is true this rose is for you.
It's me and you,
This kiss only for you.

Your beauty so rare,
My search for you,
Your heart I find,
My dream to be,
You to be mine.

My heart for you,
Only one to give,
Your hopes, your dreams,
My love to give.
I hope for you to be mine.

A rose to give,
This one for you,
A smile to receive,
Many more just from me.
Maybe you will be the one for me.

I see skies of blue,
Red roses too,
A yellow moon, bright stars,
All special,
Just like you.

A heart so blue,
Now without you,
The man to be,
I hope you see the one to be,
The one for you just for me.

The one of your dreams,
A special man for you,
The one for you the one for me,
I hope you see the man for you.
Could it be, maybe it's me?

Chapter in Life

A story to tell,
A blank page yet to fill,
Cover to cover,
One hopes to fill.

This is a story,
A story to tell,
Open the book,
Pen in hand.

No ink spilled,
Pages to fill,
So it starts,
Once upon a time.

A page is done,
A day at a time,
To fill them all,
One by one.

A chapter to start,
A year or two,
Now pages fill,
More and more left behind.

To tell the story
With hopes and dreams,
A life of love yet to live,
A happy ending still to find.

Sometimes happy,
Sometimes sad,
For life has a story,
It soon will tell.

Verse by verse,
Page by page,
The meaning of life,
To share with you.

Visions of old
Fills the book,
The future is bright,
A story to unfold.

With the past behind,
Today we know,
Now was then,
We find us here again.

Friends and family,
Characters unfold,
Some we knew,
A long time ago.

A ring to show I love you,
So it is, an "I do" too,
A family with love,
Spread over years.

My fairytale is you,
A Queen to me
You will always be,
You by my side.

I your King,
Never to let you down,
Always with you,
Never to have a frown.

The pages fill,
The chapters grow,
A book filled with love,
So the story goes.

Wonder when's
To wonder who's,
The years go by,
The book grows wise.

Pages turned,
Remember when's,
Share our memories,
For hours on end.

Since the first page,
Memories made
Of you and me
Still to be.

With pages to fill,
A happy smile
And I love you
I never would have lived without you.

A scar or two,
A storybook of you,
Not always as planned,
Never to let each other down.

Forever is near,
But very clear,
Time grows near,
I love you My Dear.

With one last page,
The book soon full,
My story told,
What a book that did unfold.

To close the book,
I set it down,
I close my eyes,
With one last look.

Book by my side,
The cover I found,
A chapter in life,
You're the one that never let me down.

C. D. Boyden

A Heart that Is True

To find a heart that is true
I wish for you.
Can't quite reach you.
How lucky I will be to find you.

A heart so true,
Mine for you,
Always true to you,
I wish to keep you.

I rest my head,
I close my eyes,
My dreams soon will be,
Every night I come to see, you and me.

Day in day out,
Every second every chance,
To think of you,
As if you were, my last chance.

Now I say, "I love you".
Like a dream come true.
Is it really you?
My love my life.

When I wake you are near,
That you may even be here,
Your heart next to mine,
A dream I will find.

The thought of you as part of me,
Now one of you with one of me,
Now complete as it is meant to be,
Our hearts will always be, you and me.

Adore

The person you are,
Happy or sad,
From love at first sight,
I adore you.

If I was a genie
With the power to give,
To grant your every last wish,
I adore you.

We go for a ride.
Sometimes you drive a little too slow,
Maybe even a little too fast,
I adore you.

I see you smile.
You make me laugh.
You fill my heart.
I adore you.

Before I sleep,
When I wake,
My first thought, always of you.
I adore you.

In the middle of the night,
When I can't sleep,
A peck on the cheek,
I adore you.

With sleep in your eyes,
When you wake,
When a cup of coffee is at stake,
I adore you.

With a smile or a frown,
A tear on your cheek,
A kiss or two to fix the leak,
I adore you.

Near or far,
A picture from you,
Always brings me next to you,
I adore you.

If today never ends,
Tomorrow never comes,
If you're not here,
I adore you.

I wake to day,
First thought of you,
To your smile,
adore you

Every minute of every day,
You love me more,
I love you the same!
I adore you more and more each and every day!

I Wish For You

I wish for you
Every day filled with joy,
Full of happiness,
Every day a blessing.

Your thoughts of me,
I think of you
Unconditionally …
Every day with you!

In this life I wished,
I wish for my true love,
To trust, to miss, just for me.
My true love now for you.

In our travels,
My life with you,
Near or far,
Always… I will love just you!

Your heart is here,
Mine is near,
There with you!
All to enjoy.

Enjoy it all,
Think of me,
Smile and laugh,
Just to know my thoughts are of you.

You bring me close,
I think of you,
Think of me,
Always us, together!

But most of all,
We have our love,
Near or far,
Together forever.

Far from me, hopes to be next to me,
Every day is one day closer,
For you to be, just with me!
Always near, Always dear... I love you!

Cold without You

I travel near and far.
I dream of you,
All without you.
It's cold without you.

Another day I look for you,
A winding road,
A road to you.
It's cold without you.

A city street,
A corner store,
Still no you.
It's cold without you.

Right next door,
Around the town,
A little café.
It's cold without you.

Coast to coast,
Highs and lows,
Every day, every night.
It's cold without you.

One day soon,
Only you,
I wait for you.
It's cold without you.

My heart waits only for you,
To hold you near,
Just to say I love you!.
It's cold without you.

The perfect you,
Is you with me.
Now never will I be..
Cold without you!

Days

Days of new,
Days of old,
Days go by,
With or without you.

Days begin with a wish of you,
Days have a middle when I think of you,
Days run on end on end.
Days all end with a dream of you.

Some happy,
Some sad,
I spend my days
Wishing for you.

Days turn to weeks,
Weeks to months,
Months to years,
Now where are you?

Days are years,
Years are days,
Every day seems like forever.
Again another day without you seems like forever.

Minutes turn to hours,
Hours to days,
Every minute of every day,
Is filled with dreams of you.

I dream one day
I will find you.
The best day
Will be with you.

My life began
The day I met you.
Now with purpose,
I wish to spend all my days with only you.

Now with you,
All my years seem like days.
I spend them all with you.
Oh how I love you!

I Give to You

My love is yours!
My life is yours,
Mine to give,
I give to you.

My happiness,
My trust,
My dreams,
I give to you.

A dream come true,
My kiss good night,
My kiss good morning,
I give to you.

My beginning,
My end,
My purpose,
I give to you.

My meaning,
The way you are,
For better or worse,
I give to you.

My love,
My heart,
My soul,
I give to you.

An hour, a day,
A week, a month,
A year, my life,
I give to you.

More

In the blink of an eye
You stole my heart.
Now with you,
I love you more.

In my dreams,
Always of you,
More is enough.
I love you more.

Your magic touch,
Your amazing charm,
A special spell to say…
I love you more.

Without you,
There is no me.
I love you more than words can say.
I love you more.

In the heat of the night,
Our first kiss,
Just for you,
I love you more.

Our first fight,
To hold you tight,
To never let go,
I love you more.

Without you,
There is no more.
If I fall,
I love you more.

My true love,
When forever comes,
Forever together we will be.
I love you more.

When there is no more,
There is only you.
You are my more.
I will always love you more!!

One Last Thought

I wish for you
Love like this,
Just to give you,
My one last thought.

My first kiss,
My life I live,
For only you,
My one last thought.

Precious time,
Never lost,
Every day I give to you,
My one last thought.

A smile, a thought,
A happy dance,
My heart I give,
My one last thought.

C. D. Boyden

No time to lose,
I hold your hand,
A walk in the sand,
My one last thought.

A morning alarm,
Your morning kiss,
Your cup of coffee,
My one last thought.

In my heart,
Precious you,
See your smile,
My one last thought,

Every day,
Every thought,
With all my love,
You're always my one, my one last thought!

My Purpose Is You

You give me purpose.
My life starts with you.
You have given me love,
My love for you.

A gift from you,
Love from you,
I am now a part of you,
To love you more every day.

A life on hold,
As I wait for you,
I feel so close,
Even far from you.

My one true love,
My feelings for you overflow,
Life with you forever,
My last love.

My everything,
Everything I feel for you.
I love you
Because you are you.

You are not perfect.
You are good.
You are bad.
You are perfect for me.

Just to be with you,
Just to feel,
Never to judge,
My everything is you.

I need you
In this life.
You are my happiness.
We are meant to be.

Love forever to be,
Your heart for me,
Mine for you,
Together now and forever.

Towel Meant for Two

I lay alone on the sand.
I dream of you.
I smile when I think of you.
This towel meant for two.

The sun on my face,
An ocean breeze,
A kiss just for you,
This towel meant for two.

We stroll hand in hand.
Footprints left in the sand,
Wish to lay you down,
This towel meant for two.

The waves splash down.
I wonder why
The towel half full.
This towel meant for two.

C. D. Boyden

You block my sun.
I open my eyes.
I see you smile standing alone …
This towel meant for two.

You take my hand,
A dream come true,
A smile just for you,
Half this towel is meant for you.

Wonder When

I wonder who,
Who will be,
The one for me,
I wonder when.

To think,
To dream,
All of you,
I wonder when.

Shed a tear once in a while.
A hug, a kiss,
Will make it all worthwhile.
I wonder when.

A simple call,
A simple kiss,
Just to make you smile,
I wonder when.

The touch of your hand,
The sound of your voice,
Your simple scent,
I wonder when.

A special time,
A perfect love,
For you and me,
I wonder when.

A choice to make,
Make no mistake,
Only you,
I wonder when.

I hope, I pray,
For maybe this next day
Here you will be,
For no longer will "I wonder when."

King and Queen

Now I dream
Soon to be, me the King,
You my Queen,
Hold my heart.

Care for me,
For now it is
As I dream,
My reality.

You the one,
Next to me,
You my Queen,
I your King.

Nothing more,
Nothing less,
For as it is,
As we are.

We know reign,
In our dream,
Together to be
King and Queen.

One

This is my one.
One only happens once.
My one first breath,
My one first day.

One first date,
One first kiss,
One first love.
You are my one.

One to give,
One to receive.
What more do we need?
Just one of you.

To me one is all,
All is one,
With one what matters more?
You are my one.

With one I need only you.
I don't need two.
I don't need more.
One is enough.

One and one does not make two.
You and me make one.
One heart, one soul.
You are my one.

One day with you is a lifetime.
A day with you is all I need.
No tomorrows, only now.
For now you are my one.

Live today as one,
For tomorrow may never come.
One last stand,
One last time to hold your hand.

One light burns bright
All through the night.
You keep me strong.
One day will come.

One last day,
One last minute,
One last breath,
One last kiss.

For once you are here,
Once you are gone,
There are no seconds.
There is no more, only one.

With you one is enough.
One last deal,
One last smile.
You … my one, my only one.

Dad

A look from you,
A bond now made,
You're the man to be my Dad;
Your son I will always be.

Time to share just with me,
You can't buy it or sell it,
Even forget it;
Your son I will always be.

A little boy
In the shadows just to see,
A sandbox just for me;
Your son I will always be.

My nose, my toes,
My heart, my hands,
A pilsner beer we share;
Your son I will always be.

A question from me,
Wise advice from you,
A simple "I love you";
Your son I will always be.

A hand to hold,
A tractor ride,
A bale of hay for you and me;
Your son I will always be

A trip, a fall,
Pick me up when I am down.
A simple day to spend with you;
Your son I will always be.

A card, a hug,
A simple smile,
A phone call from you;
Your son I will always be;

C. D. Boyden

Near or far,
At work or play,
A man to be, just like you;
Your son I will always be.

A round of golf,
Between you and me,
Crack a beer or maybe three;
Your son I will always be.

Big trucks are sold,
In search of gold.
It has to be;
Your son I will always be.

A reunion to share with family and friends,
A hay ride with you,
The family tree;
Your son I will always be.

You're my Dad,
You will always be.
No one can take that away from me;
Your son I will always be.

Days Gone By

It all starts
From days gone by,
A success or two,
A success meant for you.

All days gone by,
So far without you,
Life goes on,
A dear friend just for you.

A rose for you,
With an *I need you*;
Were do I find you?
My heart meant for you.

A failure or two,
All meant so I can find you.
Yesterday now behind.
The days go by.

Destiny is tomorrow.
To turn the corner,
Cross the road,
As days go by.

Right now all alone,
I sit and wonder why.
I look in the sky,
A dream or two, all of you.

Where are you?
Now I fly.
I never found you.
Now it's too late.

Fleeting chance,
I change my mind,
A life yet to live,
A heart full of love yet to give.

I choose to stay,
Now I am back,
To stay with you,
All my days meant for you.

A choice is made:
I know it's you,
A life with you,
When days go by.

All days go by,
Just as they always did.
Now I look back,
With an *I love you*.

Now there is a life,
A life to live,
A life for us now to live.
Days go by us together, now and forever!

C. D. Boyden

You Were My Dream

I wake today knowing
Yesterday you were my dream.
Today you are my reality.
Tomorrow you are my future.

No worries, no problems,
Tomorrow will come.
Happy or sad,
I will always choose you.

Our emotions, our reactions, we control
Others, we do not.
Together we make the choice
To love and to live.

The choice is ours
Happy or sad, mad or glad.
We share our love
For we have us.

A destiny for two
To share our thoughts, hopes and dreams,
Always all of you.
Now together, together forever.

A Day Alone

Waiting patiently,
Thoughts of you,
I open my heart;
I spend another day alone.

I keep my eyes open,
I turn the corner, I look for you,
Dream of you;
Yet I spend another day alone.

A warm smile,
A kind word I hope to hear from you,
A *Hi* or *Hello* just from you;
I spend another day alone.

Just to find you,
The woman for me,
My lifelong friend;
Yet I spend another day alone

My hope to lift you up,
With you in my life,
My heart to be yours;
Yet I spend another day alone.

One day when it is right
You will find me.
Till then...
I spend the day alone.

C. D. Boyden

You Take Me There

At night when I am alone
With thoughts of you,
You take me home.
I miss you when I am alone.

With the ring of the phone,
To hear your voice,
A gentle tone,
You take me there.

To walk with you,
Hold your hand,
The smell of your hair,
You take me there.

You're in my heart,
A tender touch.
To dream your name.
You take me there.

I close my eyes,
See you in Paris
or maybe Rome.
You take me there.

I lay you down,
A kiss on the lips.
I tuck you in.
You take me there.

A bedtime story,
A fairy tale of two,
A heart to find,
You take me there.

Good night, God bless,
Sweet, sweet dreams.
Dream tonight of what tomorrow will bring.
You take me there.

You Didn't Have to Be

You were the Dad you didn't have to be.
You made me who I am today.
I do the things I do because of you.
I've seen you when you didn't see me.

I learned from you when you weren't teaching.
I see things today with your vision.
I do the things I've done because you were there.
I am me because of you.
You were the man I always wanted to be.
You were the Dad you didn't have to be.

The tone of your voice,
A gentle smile,
A funny joke,
Or lend me a smoke!
You were the Dad you didn't have to be.

I was your shadow.
You were my hero,
The man I wanted to be.
You were my Dad but you didn't have to be.

We drove big trucks.
We had big dreams.
We followed long roads,
Some never traveled,
But none forgotten.
You were my Dad because you chose to be.
I am your son because you chose me!

Found You

Lost to me,
Now you're found.
Gone so long,
In this life I found.

The one for me,
A dream come true,
Since I found you,
Never want to be without you.

I wish, I wait,
Where are you?
I pray, I dream,
I hope for you.

The day will come,
Patiently await,
Love I missed,
Yet to have.

My one true love,
This one I found.
Far from here,
Now she is near.

Yours and mine,
This is our time,
Memories to make,
Memories to share.

We travel near,
We travel far,
A journey for two,
This life meant for me with you.

Two paths to cross,
A place for you,
A place for me,
Here together always forever.

My heart I give,
I give to you.
All my love I share,
I share with you.

C. D. Boyden

Her Man to Find

To live in a land
With no man,
A choice to make,
Alone she must go.

A woman with love,
A precious gift yet to give,
A man to find,
The world to explore.

Now alone, she closes her eyes
To dream of him,
A smile to see,
So happy she will be.

A missing piece,
A heart to fill,
A prince to find,
But all in good time.

Near or far,
A trail left behind,
For her to find,
She will take the chance.

Now to search,
She goes alone,
With no fear,
Of what lays ahead.

The journey begins,
She leaves all behind,
Family and friends,
Castles and crowns,

A dream to love,
To feel, to touch,
To give, to receive,
To have, to hold.

Her man to find,
The dream of him,
Their magic to share,
Forever together, two as a pair.

Your Love I Find

Your love I find,
Still yet to define,
Two souls as one,
Pasts gone by.

Now united
For the first time,
As if lost,
Never to find.

God provides
The path for two.
For now I found you,
The dream comes true.

The light is bright,
The past behind,
The future we hold,
Two hearts are true.

My Dear how I love you
For I always knew I would find you.
A trail of tears now left behind,
Years lost, a future we find.

We carry forward,
Life's gone by,
Not totally forgotten,
But left behind.

Now it begins,
The life for two;
It starts a new.
I know I love you.

The old left behind,
Now all new.
Our souls are two,
Two now as one.

In this life
I walk with you
As if I always knew you,
Every day brand new.

Life is not chance,
But a path now found.
The path we follow
Has led me to you.

As is as once was,
A heart so true,
I never knew
How much I could love you.

The chance we take,
Two as a pair, together we share,
The life we will live, for now it begins,
Love now was never lost, only found!

Reasons Not to Run ...

1. If it feels right ... It probably is ... Go with it! (Even if you're scared.)
2. To laugh so hard together it makes your face hurt.
3. The way I look at you.
4. The butterflies from a text message.
5. You're the last thing on my mind at the end of the day.
6. The first thing on my mind every morning.
7. Someone to share special kisses with.
8. A shoulder when you need one.
9. A hug because you deserve one.
10. Will pick you up when you're down.
11. Someone to lay next to you on a rainy day.
12. To share a look between two.
13. To know I get you.
14. Midnight phone calls that last for hours.
15. I can hold your hand like no other can.
16. Someone to miss when we are apart.
17. To open your heart.
18. To open your mind.
19. It is nice to know someone cares that much about you.
20. You make me smile from the inside out!

21. I can carry heavy things for you.

22. I can open the pickle jar for you.

23. You deserve the best.

24. Just to make you smile.

25. Maybe you think I am OK …

26. Made you smile when you felt like crying …